Mum cook book

25 good reasons to use babycook
before your baby arrives

Author and design
Virginie Michelin

Photographer
Françoise Nicol

Health advice
by Paule Neyrat

BÉABA

Contents

craving

for care

Craving
for freshness

Craving
for (great) flavors

Béaba...

Since 1989, the year that babycook was created, Béaba has been revolutionizing the child care market by developing innovative and ingenious designs. Béaba has also simplified parents' lives by finding solutions suited to their everyday needs.

Each product is designed with them in mind and to meet their expectations of function and style. For parents' peace of mind, Béaba is also the first French manufacturer to have removed Bisphenol A from its products.

With babycook you can give your baby the best of a diversified diet.

It steam cooks everything in less than 15 minutes. Béaba, the art of living with a baby...

More information at www.beaba.com and more tips at www.beablog.fr

babycook and babycook accessories

babycook bag

The perfect accessory for taking your babycook with you for the weekend or on vacation...

babycook scale

Weigh your ingredients to the nearest gram/ounce.

babycook seasoning ball

Add flavor to your dishes! This ball adds taste to your baby's food without leaving a trace.

maxi and baby portion sets

For storing, freezing and reheating food.

babycook pasta/rice-cooker

Cook pasta, rice and grains without fuss.

multiportions

This clever invention provides you with individual molds for your purées and compotes.

The *babycook book*, lets you stimulate your baby's taste buds, while the *kid cook book*, lets you make dishes your children will love to eat!

Virginie's
basic rules

Your life changes when you're expecting a baby – your feelings, what you feel like doing and... even what's on your plate! To begin with, you are strongly advised to avoid certain foods for your own good and that of your baby. To make things worse, during this 9-month period, your favorite food might turn your stomach, while, on the contrary, new irrational and, at times, uncontrollable cravings may appear.

Don't worry, you are an absolutely normal mom-to-be!

As a mother of three, I know what it's like to be standing in front of the refrigerator when the cravings creep in and not know what to do. How can I find the food or a dish I'm allowed to have that is balanced and that can satisfy my momentary urge?

To make life easier for you, I've prepared 25 recipes suited to your needs and urges: they are simple, healthy, nutritionally balanced and delicious.

My advice
for expectant moms

1 GIVE IN TO YOUR CRAVINGS, EVEN THE WEIRDEST ONES

Do your cravings seem irrational? This is completely normal. Don't think twice about eating whatever your body is asking for: sweet, savory, sour, bitter, spicy... Naturally, you have to set reasonable limits and stick to the list of ingredients your doctor will have told you to avoid.

Always keep in mind that babies discover flavors in the womb. Their sense of taste can be developed by eating as wide a range of food as possible during pregnancy. That will make life much easier when it comes to introducing your growing child to new kinds of food. For instance, when I was expecting my first child, I became obsessed with highly seasoned dishes. When he was only one year old, he was already devouring the spiciest food!

2 WATCH YOUR NUTRITIONAL BALANCE

Indulge your food cravings, but don't forget to keep an eye on your weight during your pregnancy. Of course, you can lose the extra pounds afterwards, but be aware that your body has a memory: the more weight you gain during these nine months, the harder it will be to stabilize it later. Don't forget that after giving birth, you will want to get back into shape as soon as possible and update your wardrobe. If you put on too much weight, the only thing you can guarantee will be depression!

ENJOY YOURSELF

3 My last piece of advice as a mother: take care of yourself during your pregnancy. Slow things down and move in tune with your body. Learn to delegate; your family and friends are there to help you. Relax and enjoy yourself; that way you will be a relaxed and radiant mom.

Ultimately, pregnancy only really lasts a short time so make the most of it. Despite some inconvenience and the sacrifices you'll need to make, it's a special time for you and your child.

Practical nutritional
advice

PREGNANCY ISN'T A FLU THAT LASTS NINE MONTHS; IN OTHER WORDS, IT ISN'T AN ILLNESS. YOU ARE CREATING A LITTLE BUNDLE OF JOY THAT WILL DRIVE YOU CRAZY, BUT YOUR BODY WAS MADE FOR THIS. SO DON'T PANIC! LISTEN TO YOUR BODY; IT AND THE PERSON GROWING INSIDE WILL GUIDE YOU. THIS WILL HELP YOU TO MAKE GOOD FOOD CHOICES.

● EATING FOR TWO?

Don't! That's the best way to put on 50 pounds when gaining 20-25 is the norm. Your energy requirements are the same in the first trimester. They increase by 200 calories in the second and by 400 in the third to satisfy those of the baby growing inside you. There's no need to count every single calorie; you'll feel hungrier and you'll eat a little more. But you can eat anything because eating a little of everything slowly is the key to a balanced diet. You'll also need a small snack, besides your three obligatory meals.

● EAT FOR YOURSELF AND THE BABY

That's right! Because your baby is growing inside you and needs to grow more, if you don't gradually build up reserves, you won't have the strength to hold him or her in your arms. Your baby's bones are growing, meaning a greater need for calcium, magnesium and proteins. You'll need to eat yogurt or dairy products with every meal and hard rind cheeses (the richest in calcium) from time to time. Drink bottled water that is rich in magnesium: the French brands Hépar®, Contrex®, Rozana® and Quézac® are a good source. They also have a high calcium content, which is good, and they don't have any extra calories. Dairy products also provide you with protein in addition to calcium. You'll also need a lot of iron and Vitamin B9 (to prevent malformation). Normally, your doctor will prescribe you supplements; that's how it works. Even so, don't miss out on meat, especially red meat, which is richest in iron, or on vegetables, particularly leafy greens, which are the richest in folate (Vitamin B9).

● THINK ABOUT YOUR BABY'S BRAIN

So that your baby's cells, especially those of the nervous system, develop well, you need Omega 3. For this, you should eat oily fish (organic salmon, sardines and mackerel) at least 3 times a week and use rapeseed (Canola) oil on a regular basis. Fish also gives you iodine, which is essential for your baby's growth and intellectual development. And logically, don't drink alcohol! It goes without saying that you will have given up smoking after your pregnancy test...or sooner.

What should you drink?
Water, water and more water! You can have it still or sparkling (except if you feel bloated). Infusions, fruit and vegetable juices and smoothies are fine. But careful with coffee and tea; the caffeine they contain may irritate the little one.

● MORNING SICKNESS?

Half of pregnant women suffer from nausea, no one really knows why. Is it from hormones or stress? If you suffer from it, eat little and often, whenever you feel hungry, and eat as little fat as possible. Don't force anything down that could make you throw up. Try ginger; it's known to calm nausea: chew it freshly sliced or grate it and make infusions. If you eat dried ginger, limit your intake to 1/15 oz per day. Acupressure bands for morning sickness (available at pharmacies) are also useful and are risk free. This is not the case of anti-emetic drugs, which, like all drugs, can have a teratogenic effect (harmful to your unborn baby).

● CONSTIPATED?

The more your baby grows, the more your colon is compressed. Now is not the time to miss out on dietary fiber (vegetables and wholegrain cereal) or water, which is what usually causes this problem, whether you're pregnant or not. Don't take laxatives as they can be aggressive; but do eat prunes – there's nothing better. And yogurts with Lactobacillus Bifidus aren't bad either.

● TOXOPLASMOSIS AND LISTERIA

If you've never been inoculated for toxoplasmosis (the test is compulsory in France), then you should keep away from cats. You'll also need to abstain from eating raw food (the nasty toxoplasma parasite is destroyed at 151°F) and use gloves when gardening. Many animals are infected with it and they leave their droppings on the ground.

If you don't want to suffer from listeria, a bacterial disease transmitted by Listeria monocytogenes and which can have devastating effects on you, don't eat raw milk cheeses or the rind of soft cheese (such as

Camembert), or deli products such as paté and rillettes. This sort of food is most easily infected. But they are too fattening anyway! Wash your hands often and keep your refrigerator extremely clean.

This needn't involve drama, just a few precautions, which you should continue when you breastfeed your beautiful baby. The main thing is to enjoy the happiness this pregnancy brings you.

Paule Neyrat, dietitian

for care

Petit-suisse cheese
with berries and cereal

For 1 mom
Preparation time: 5 minutes

1 1.75-oz **tubs of Petit Suisse or cottage cheese**
1.75-oz **crunchy muesli with berries**
20 **red currants**
1.75-oz **raspberries**
1 tbsp **turbinado sugar**

Virginie

My breakfast ritual!
Alternate raw and cooked fruit depending
on what you feel like and the season:
apples, pears, strawberries... You can also
try crunchy cereal with chocolate chips!

Paule

You can easily increase the amount of fruit.
Your daily intake should be a minimum of
10.5 oz.
Add a slice of wholegrain bread (for slow
carbs to stop your cravings).

1. Process the cereal with the berries in the babycook bowl.
2. Arrange the Petit Suisse cheese, the fresh berries and the powdered cereal on a plate. Sprinkle with sugar and enjoy.

Variation: *You can also make a berry coulis. Fill the reservoir of your babycook with 2 measures of water and steam part of the fruit for 10 minutes. Then blend the fruit with sugar to taste.*

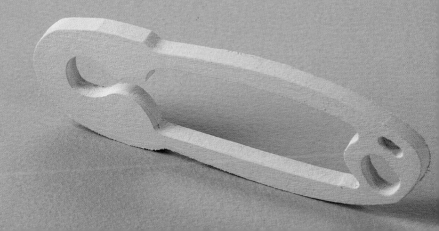

Dried fruit
cinnamon nibbles

For 9 cinnamon nibbles
Preparation time: 10 minutes
Cooking time: 10 minutes

2 tbsp **rolled oats**
1 1.75-oz **tub of Petit Suisse or cottage cheese**
1 **egg**
2 **dried figs**
2 **dried apricots**
1 tbsp **dried cranberries**
1 tbsp **cinnamon powder**

1. Preheat the oven to 325°F.
2. Process the rolled oats in the babycook to make a powder.
3. Put the powder in a bowl with the Petit Suisse cheese, egg, figs, dried apricots, cranberries and cinnamon.
4. Fill a silicone mini-muffin mold tray with the mixture. Bake in the oven for 10 minutes.
5. Enjoy the nibbles for breakfast or as a snack during the day. Keep them in an airtight container.

Variation: you can replace the rolled oats with oat bran, which you can find at supermarkets and health food or organic food stores.

Virginie

It is easy to get addicted to these warm little things! They're also delicious in a savory version: just replace the dried fruit with a Laughing Cow® cheese wedge and some ham.

Paule

This way the cinnamon nibbles will have more proteins but fewer minerals. Why not alternate!

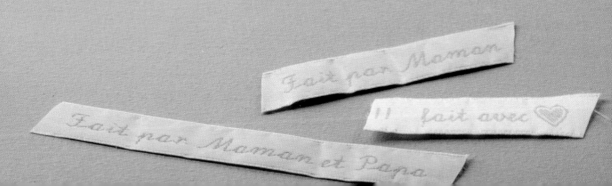

Garlic crème

For 1 mom
Preparation time: 10 minutes
Cooking time: 20 minutes

10 oz garlic cloves that have been peeled and
        the germ removed (about 3 heads)
5 oz (about 2/3 cup) vegetable stock
4 tbsp cream (soy or cow's milk)
1 tbsp slivered almonds

Virginie

*This healthy white dish won't give you
bad breath!*

Paule

*Garlic is actually beneficial for the
cardiovascular system (among other
things, it lowers blood pressure).
It's also anti-bacterial, anti-allergenic
and anti-oxidant.*

1. Fill the reservoir of your babycook with 3 measures of water. Place the garlic cloves in the steam basket
   and cook for 20 minutes.
2. After steaming, blend the garlic together with the vegetable stock and the cream. Sprinkle the slivered
   almonds over it and serve hot.

Two-carrot
savory puddings

For 2 puddings
Preparation time: 15 minutes
Cooking time: 25 minutes

1 **small yellow carrot**
1 **small orange carrot**
2 **eggs**
4 fl oz (1/2 cup) **light cream or soy cream**
1 tsp **cumin**
Salt
Pepper

1. Preheat the oven to 325°F.
2. Wash and peel the carrots. Use the vegetable peeler to make carrot ribbons.
3. Fill the reservoir of your babycook with 3 measures of water. Place the carrot ribbons in the steam basket and cook for 10 minutes. Once steamed, place the carrot ribbons in 2 ovenproof ramekins.
4. Mix the eggs with the cream, cumin, salt and pepper in a bowl. Then pour the mixture gently into the ramekins.
5. Bake in the oven for 15 minutes.

Virginie

If you feel like cheese, add some Boursin ail et fines herbes® (garlic and fine herb cheese) to the egg mixture.

Paule

Two puddings will practically cover your protein intake for this meal. Have some fish or meat if you feel like it, but it isn't necessary, as you will more than likely end the meal with a dairy product.

Citrus
scallops

For 1 mom
Preparation time: 20 minutes
Cooking time: 20 minutes

5 **large scallops**
1/2 **pink grapefruit**
1 **orange**
2 tbsp **sugar**
1 sheet **of nori (optional, available in the Asian food section of supermarkets)**

Virginie

If you are worried about the freshness of the scallops, use frozen ones and adapt the cooking time to the instructions on the packet.

Paule

Use citrus fruit that hasn't been treated after harvesting, or organic fruit. If you don't, you'll be absorbing thiabendazole, ortho-phenylphenol and benomyl (products used to make them shiny and last longer) and your baby doesn't need any of them, not even in tiny doses.

1. Scrape the zest from the fruit and set it aside in a saucepan.
2. Peel the ½ grapefruit and separate the segments. Place half of the segments in the saucepan and set aside the remainder on a plate.
3. Cut the orange in two. Squeeze the juice from the first half and pour it into the saucepan. Peel the second half. Separate it into segments and place them on the plate.
4. Add the sugar to the saucepan and reduce it for 15 minutes until you obtain a syrup. Strain through a sieve.
5. Cut out the nori sheet and place it under the steam basket so as to infuse the scallops with its flavor without staining them. Fill the reservoir of the babycook with 2 measures of water. Place the scallops in the steam basket and cook for about 3 minutes.
6. Serve the scallops on the plate with the citrus pieces and drizzle with the sauce.

Morning
sickness infusion

For 1 mom
Preparation time: 5 minutes
Cooking time: 1 hour

1 oz **fresh ginger**
1 tbsp **turbinado sugar**
1 cup **boiling water**

1. Peel the ginger root, cut it into small pieces and purée it in the babycook. Add a little water if necessary to obtain a fine texture. Boil the water.
2. Put the ginger purée into a small teapot with the sugar and pour 1 cup of boiling water over it. Leave it for 1 hour to infuse.
3. Drink this ginger infusion every 4 hours to prevent nausea. You can also mix it with fruit juice or green tea.

Tip: if you want to prevent nausea, you should also eat several small meals throughout the day.

Virginie

Even if morning sickness often only occurs in the first 3 months, it's awful! This recipe is used by Antillean women and it's really effective.

Paule

The effect ginger has on nausea has been proven scientifically and is documented in a number of medical studies. It helps with digestion and also has anti-inflammatory properties and is packed full of minerals.

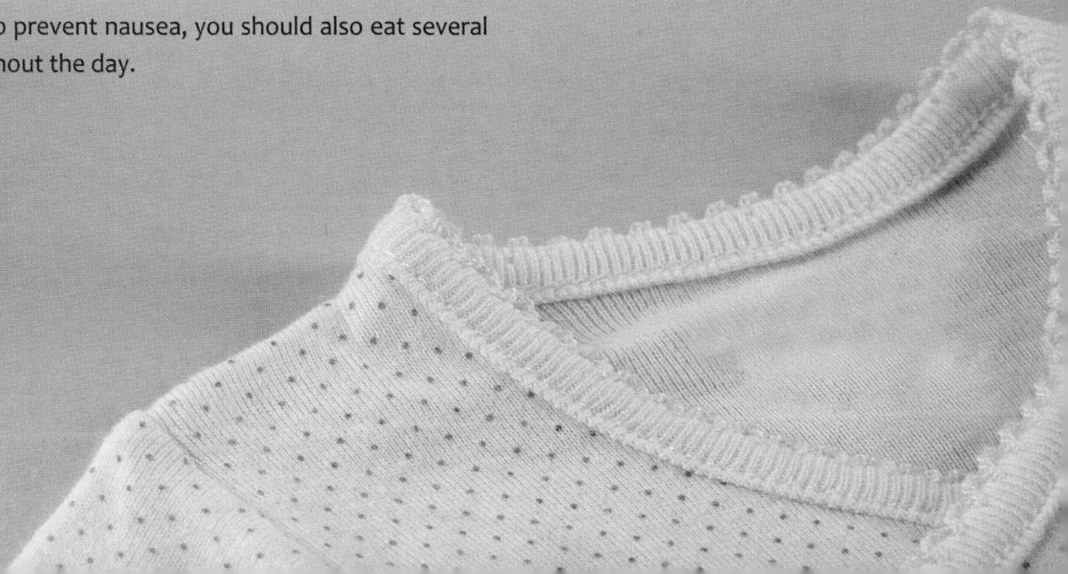

Fruits of the forest smoothie

For 1 mom
Preparation time: 5 minutes

7 oz fresh or frozen fruits of the forest (mixed berries)
**1 pint of cow's milk, almond milk or rice milk (available
in the health food section of supermarkets or in
organic food stores)**
1 tbsp agave nectar (optional)

1. Blend the fruit, milk and agave nectar together in the babycook.
2. Enjoy your freshly-made smoothie.

Virginie

*This is delicious with buttermilk and
with stone fruit: apricot, peach and
nectarine, and even banana to give
it a thicker texture...*

Paule

*If the fruit is very ripe, the agave nectar
won't be necessary. Plant milks don't
contain calcium, so don't forget to have
yogurt or cottage cheese during the day.*

Beauty
Masks

For 1 mom
Preparation time: 5 minutes

Virginie

Because we're worth it, don't you agree?

Paule

Naturally!

Wash and dry your face. Blend together the ingredients for the mask in the babycook and apply the preparation to your face and neck. Leave it for 20 minutes. Lie down and take advantage of this time to unwind... Rinse it off with running water.

Vitamin mask for a fruity complexion

Dice 2 dried apricots and place the cubes in the babycook steam basket. Fill the reservoir with 2 measures of water and pour 2 oz of boiling water over the apricots. Cook for 10 minutes before blending and leaving it to cool. Apply it to your face.

Moisturizing mask

Blend one ripe avocado in your babycook with 1 tbsp extra virgin olive oil (organic if possible).

Mask for dry skin

Blend 3 tbsp pollen (available in the health food section of supermarkets or organic food stores) in the babycook. Then add an egg yolk. Blend again.

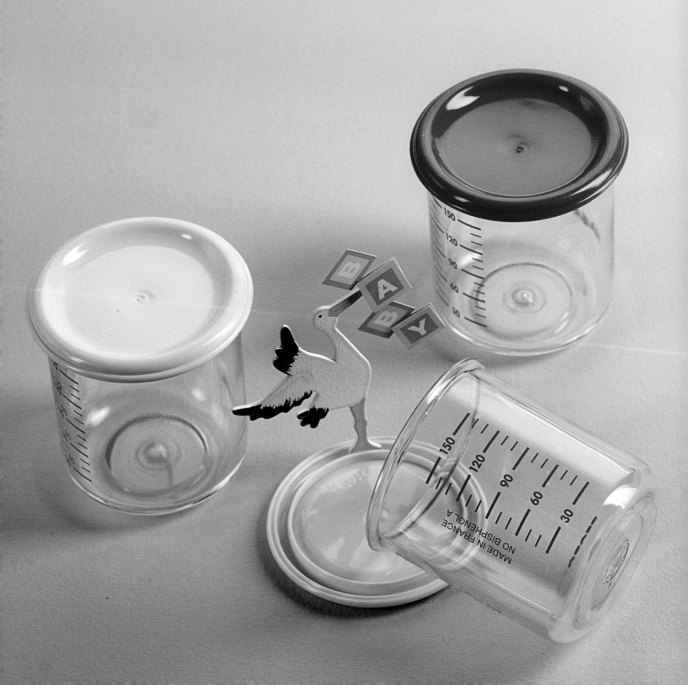

for freshness

Vegetable
sandwiches

For 3 sandwiches
Preparation time: 20 minutes
Cooking time: 12 minutes

6 slices of **wholegrain bread (or 7-grain bread)**
3.5 oz **unpeeled zucchini**
1.75 oz **unpeeled eggplant**
1.75 oz **yellow bell pepper**
1.75 oz **red bell pepper**
0.7 oz **pine nuts**
1 oz **sun-dried tomatoes in oil**
3.5 oz **cottage cheese**
4 tsp **mint sauce**

1. Dice the zucchini, eggplant and peppers into 1/8-inch cubes. Use an Alligator® vegetable dicer if you have one. Fill the reservoir of your babycook with 2 measures of water and place the vegetables in the steam basket. Cook for 10 minutes.
2. In the meantime, toast the pine nuts in a dry non-stick frying pan. Cut the dried tomatoes into little pieces and mix the cottage cheese with the mint sauce.
3. When the vegetables are cooked, place them in a bowl. Add the dried tomatoes and 1 tsp of oil from the jar they came in and mix. Leave to cool.
4. Spread the cottage cheese over the slices of bread and make sandwiches with the mixed vegetables and pine nuts.

Virginie

Are you craving something sweet? Replace the mint sauce with 1.75 oz pasteurized goat's milk yogurt and the 1/2 oz of wholegrain mustard with 3/4 oz of cherry jelly. Add fresh basil to your vegetables and use a corn tortilla.

Paule

The bread has fiber, carbohydrates and a little protein; the vegetables have a little carbohydrate and lots of minerals and anti-oxidants; and the cottage cheese has proteins and calcium. It's everything you need!

Rainbow
tomato salad

For 1 mom
Preparation time: 15 minutes

Green Zebra tomato
yellow cherry tomatoes
orange cherry tomatoes
Black Krim tomato (or Heirloom tomato)
red Cœur de Pigeon tomatoes (or pear tomatoes)
small bunch of basil
olive oil mixed with rapeseed (Canola) oil
pasteurized feta cheese
white balsamic vinegar
pumpkin and sunflower seed mix

Virginie

You can replace the feta cheese with pasteurized buffalo mozzarella and add fresh herbs: chervil, chives, tarragon... I love this salad because it's a treat for both the tastebuds and the eyes!

Paule

There are plenty of antioxidants in the tomatoes and Omega 3 in the different oils. It's all good! Don't worry about overdoing the herbs: they're full of minerals and beneficial vitamins.

Pluck the basil leaves and blend them with the oil in your babycook to obtain a runny green mixture.
Prepare the dressing: crumble the feta coarsely in a bowl. Add the basil oil and the balsamic vinegar and mix gently.
Wash the tomatoes. Cut the cherry tomatoes in halves, the Green Zebra in slices and the Black Krim in quarters.
Pour the dressing over and sprinkle with pumpkin and sunflower seeds.

Tip: Today it's easy to find trays of cherry or Cœur de Pigeon tomatoes in every color. However, green or black tomatoes are mainly found in markets or at your local fruitier, greengrocer or farmer's market.

Cold
cucumber and green apple soup

For 1 mom
Preparation time: 10 minutes

5-6.75 fl oz (2/3-3/4 cup) very cold drinking yogurt
1/2 cucumber
1 organic Granny Smith apple
1 tbsp lime juice
1 tbsp argan or linseed oil
A few mint leaves

Virginie

Real concentrated freshness for summer,
this soup can be made with any
apple variety.

Paule

Cucumber is easier to digest when blended
rather than sliced. Linseed (flaxseed) oil
contains more Omega 3 (essential fatty
acids that are so often lacking) than
argan oil.

1. Peel the cucumber, remove the seeds and cut it into chunks. Cut the Granny Smith apple in quarters. Remove the stalk and seeds but leave the skin if you use an organic apple.
2. Put the cucumber chunks, the apple quarters, the lime juice and the drinking yogurt in the babycook bowl. Blend together until you obtain a smooth soup.
3. When serving, add the teaspoonful of oil and decorate with chopped mint leaves, and with thin strips of apple if you like a crunchy texture.

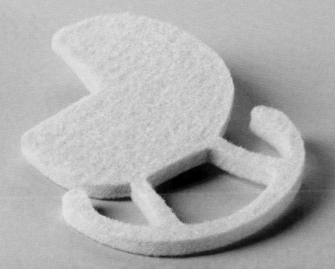

Bulgur wheat salad
with dried fruit

Virginie

I love the many flavors and textures of this salad. I sometimes replace the ewe's milk cheese with Beaufort d'été or fruity-tasting Comté cheese.

Paule

The hazelnuts, figs, grapes and dried cranberries provide a good dose of minerals, particularly magnesium.

For 1 mom
Preparation time: 10 minutes
Cooking time: 15 minutes

4.5 oz **bulgur wheat**
10 **green grapes**
10 **hazelnuts**
3 **dried figs**
1/2 **apple**
2 oz **ewe's milk cheese (or sheep's milk cheese)**
1 tbsp **raisins**
1 tbsp **dried cranberries vinaigrette made from cider vinegar and grapeseed**

1. Fill the reservoir of your babycook with 3 measures of water. Place the bulgur wheat in the rice-cooker accessory and cook for 15 minutes. Leave it to cool.
2. Cut the grapes and hazelnuts in half. Dice the dried figs, the apple and the cheese.
3. Add the cheese and the fresh and dried fruit to the wheat and dress with the vinaigrette.

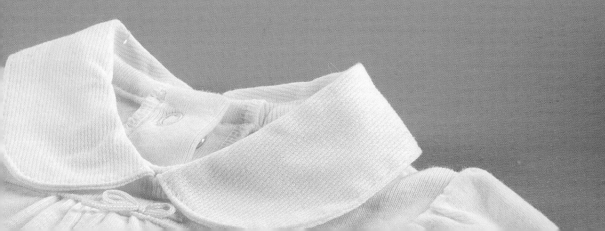

Curd cheese
and vegetable pudding

For 1 mom
Preparation time: 20 minutes
Cooking time: 10 minutes
Refrigeration time: 3 hours

1.75 oz curd cheese or Greek yogurt
1 oz radish
1.75 oz fresh or frozen peas
1.75 oz fresh or frozen peeled fava beans
1/3 envelop powdered gelatin
3 tbsp cream
Enough cucumber or spinach to garnish

Virginie

You can flavor this pudding with fresh mint and add sliced black radish or diced cucumber.

Paule

Drink the liquid from the curd cheese – it's full of calcium! If you have a tendency to gain a lot of weight, use light or single cream, which has less fat.

1. Wash and peel the radishes and slice them finely.
2. Fill the reservoir of your babycook with 3 measures of water. Place the peas and fava beans in the steam basket and cook them for 10 minutes. After this time, immerse them in iced water to stop the cooking and so that they keep their green color.
3. Mix the curd cheese gently with the radish, beans and peas in a small mixing bowl.
4. Heat the cream and reserve it. Sprinkle the powdered gelatin evenly over the surface of 1/4 cup of water, allowing it to stand for about 5 minutes for the gelatin to soften. Add the gelatin and liquid mixture to the still hot (but not boiling) cream, stirring until they have dissolved completely.
5. Pour the cream over the curd cheese and vegetables and mix everything until it is even.
6. Line a large ramekin with plastic wrap and pour in the mixture. Refrigerate the pudding for 3 hours.
7. Take the pudding out of the mold and serve it with cucumber or spinach.

Fish terrine

For 1 terrine
Preparation time: 30 minutes
Cooking time: 7 minutes
Refrigeration time: 1 hour

6.25 oz **filleted organic salmon**
5.25 oz **filleted white fish**
1 **small zucchini**
1 **avocado**
3 tbsp **cream (soy or cow's milk)**
The juice from 1/2 a lemon
Fleur de sel (or sea salt)
Freshly ground pepper

Virginie

You can enjoy this cool recipe with a guacamole made with lots of cilantro and thinned with soy cream.

Paule

Two or three slices of this terrine with wholegrain bread, a green salad, yogurt and fruit and there you have it! This is a good and easy-to-make meal that gives you everything you need: protein, carbohydrates, fat, vitamins and minerals.

1. Use a vegetable peeler to make zucchini ribbons.
2. Fill the reservoir of your babycook with 3 measures of water. Place the zucchini ribbons in the steaming bowl and cook them for 7 minutes.
3. Line a small terrine dish with plastic wrap, leaving a good length hanging over the edges. Line the mold with overlapping zucchini ribbons until it is completely covered.
4. Rinse the steam basket and put the fish in it. Steam it for 10 minutes.
5. Peel the avocado. Dice it and squeeze lemon juice over it.
6. Blend the salmon in the babycook, and add salt, pepper and lemon juice. Place half of it at the bottom of the terrine to form an even layer.
7. Then blend the white fish with the cream. Place half of it over the salmon.
8. Form a layer of avocado cubes, a second layer of white fish and, finally, another layer using the rest of the salmon.
9. Wrap the terrine completely with the excess plastic wrap and refrigerate for 1 hour.
10. Serve it very cold.

Special delivery

Mango
soup

For 1 mom
Preparation time: 10 minutes
Refrigeration time: 30 minutes

8 oz **coarsely chopped mango chunks**
3.5 fl oz (less than 1/2 cup) **pineapple juice**
The juice from 1/2 a lime
5 **sprigs of cilantro**

1. Put the pineapple juice and 7 oz of mango pieces in the babycook bowl. Add the lime juice and the cilantro leaves. Blend it all until you obtain a creamy soup.
2. Refrigerate it for 30 minutes until the flavors mix together.
3. Add the remaining mango pieces just before serving and enjoy the soup straight away.

Virginie

Mango is also deliciously refreshing in the savory version. Choose a very firm mango, cut it into cubes and add finely chopped shallots, cilantro or mint, lemon juice and a little rapeseed oil. Leave to marinate overnight in the refrigerator and you'll have a lovely treat.

Paule

Mango gives you a real shot of anti-oxidant carotenes. It's good for your skin and cells, and the baby's, too. Think about this fruit in winter; it's very useful.

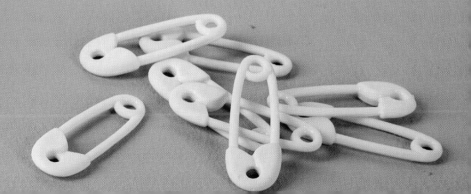

Frozen raspberry
Petit Suisse cheese pops

For 6 1.75-oz tubs of Petit Suisse cheese
Preparation time: 10 minutes
Freezing time: 3 hours

1 pack **of 6 x 1.75-oz tubs of Petit Suisse or cottage cheese**
7 oz **fresh or frozen raspberries**
4 tbsp **vanilla sugar**

Virginie

You can replace the raspberries with any raw or cooked fruit you like. Stock up on these if you have kids; they'll love them.

Paule

Dairy + fruit is always a winning combination that mixes calcium, protein and vitamins. Make this dessert with blackcurrants when in season; this fruit is really good for you.

1. Blend the fruit and sugar in the babycook until you have an even mixture. Add the 6 tubs of Petit Suisse and mix lightly to obtain a marbling effect.
2. Clean and dry the Petit Suisse tubs and pour your fruit preparation into them. Place a wooden stick or a small colored plastic spoon in the middle of each mold and freeze for 3 hours.

Tip: You can use a popsicle mold if you do not have Petite Suisse tubs.

cra ving

for (great) flavors

Crispy mini
goat's cheese rolls

Virginie

The mixture of soft and crisp is delicious. You can replace the goat's cheese rolls with mini Camembert cheeses or Crottin de Chavignol cheese halves.

Paule

Pistachios are full of minerals, anti-oxidants and fiber. The fatty acids they contain are basically unsaturated and with a high protein content. They are one of the best types of nut.

For 5 mini rolls
Preparation time: 20 minutes
Cooking time: 20 minutes

5 x 1-oz **cheese rolls made from pasteurized goat's milk**
1 **packet of Kadayif pastry (available in Middle Eastern supermarkets)**
1 oz **shelled pistachio nuts**
1 tbsp **maple syrup (or liquid honey)**

1. Preheat the oven to 350°F.
2. Chop the pistachios coarsely in the babycook and spread them out over a plate. Pour the maple syrup over another plate.
3. Roll each goat's cheese roll in maple syrup and then in the chopped pistachio to cover them. Unroll the kadayif pastry and wrap a few strings around each mini roll.
4. Place the mini rolls on a sheet tray lined with a sheet of parchment paper. Bake them for 15-20 minutes until they turn golden. Serve with a spinach salad or one made from crisp baby leaves.

Tip kadayif pastry is a ball of warka pastry strings that dry very quickly when in contact with air. It is used in many Middle Eastern desserts drizzled with honey. If you can't find any, replace it with warka or phyllo pastry cut into strips.

Duck
lasagna

For 1 mom and 1 dad
Preparation time: 30 minutes
Cooking time: 30 minutes

6 sheets of fresh lasagna cut to the size of the molds
2.5 oz carrot
1 oz celery
1 confit duck leg
7 oz fresh or frozen wild mushrooms
2.75 oz ricotta cheese
1 tbsp cream
1 tbsp turmeric
1 oz shredded cheese

Virginie

If you want a creamier white sauce, make it with wholegrain einkorn wheat or chestnut flour, which you can find at your health food store.

Paule

This is a complete and nutritionally balanced dish. There is protein in the duck and the cheese; fiber, minerals and some carbohydrates in the vegetables and mushrooms; and carbohydrates in the pasta.

1. Peel and dice the carrot and celery. Fill the reservoir of your babycook with 3 measures of water. Place the vegetable cubes in the steaming bowl and cook for 10 minutes.
2. In the meantime, heat the duck confit in a saucepan on low heat. Put a little duck fat in a frying pan. Add the mushrooms and let them cook in it for a few minutes.
3. Mix the ricotta cheese with the cream in a bowl. Add a little duck fat to give it the consistency of white sauce. Add the turmeric.
4. Bone and shred the duck leg. Mix the crumbled duck meat with the vegetables and mushrooms.
5. Place a layer of ricotta sauce at the base of the 2 individual gratin dishes followed by a lasagna sheet and a layer of duck. Repeat the process and finish with a sheet of lasagna and a layer of ricotta sauce. Cover them in shredded cheese and bake for 15 minutes.

Middle-Eastern-style
veal meatballs

For 1 mom and 1 friend
Preparation time: 20 minutes
Cooking time: 30 minutes

7 oz **veal**
3 oz **bulgur wheat (or quinoa)**
2 oz **onion**
1 tbsp **cinnamon**
1 tbsp **cumin**
1 tbsp **turmeric**
1 tbsp **honey**
0.5 oz **fresh cilantro**
1 **egg**

Virginie

Accompany these meatballs with a Middle Eastern sauce: finely chop 1 small onion and sweat it in butter on low heat. Add a handful of raisins, 1 tbsp of water, cinnamon and honey. Cook it for 3 minutes before blending in your babycook.

Paule

Quinoa is richer in plant protein and minerals (especially iron) than bulgur wheat. It isn't a cereal; instead, it's the seed of an herbaceous plant that grows in the highlands of South America and is full of nutritional goodness.

1. Fill the reservoir of your babycook with 3 measures of water. Put the bulgur in the babycook rice-cooker accessory and cook for 20 minutes.
2. In the meantime, cut the meat into chunks and peel the onion. When the bulgur is cooked, chop the onion finely in the babycook bowl. Add the meat, spices, fresh cilantro and honey. Process again and transfer the mixture to a mixing bowl. Add the whole egg and the bulgur and mix it all together.
3. Make a dozen walnut-size meatballs. Shallow fry them in olive oil for 10 minutes, turning them regularly.
4. Decorate them with chopped cilantro and eat.

Pear and Mimolette tart

Virginie

Mature Mimolette is certainly better but you should choose young cheese if you want to slice it finely.

Paule

Young Mimolette is a little less fatty than the mature so it's good. And it's great for calcium!

For 1 tart
Preparation time: 20 minutes
Cooking time: 30 minutes
Standing time: 30 minutes

1 or 2 **pears**
4.5 oz **Mimolette cheese or other cow's milk cheese**
1.75 oz **soft butter**
3.5 oz (less than 1/2 cup) **all-purpose flour**
Salt
Fresh thyme

1. Blend 1.75 oz of Mimolette cheese in the babycook bowl and set it aside.
2. Mix the butter with the flour and salt in a mixing bowl. Knead it to form a ball. Add the blended cheese and leave the dough to stand covered in plastic wrap.
3. Preheat the oven to 350°F.
4. Grease a 20-cm/8 inch cake mold with butter and flour. Flatten the dough with a rolling pin and line the mold with it. Prick the dough with a fork, cover it with parchment paper and cover it with dry beans. Pre-cook it for 10 minutes in the bottom part of the oven. Leave it to cool outside the oven.
5. Peel the pears. Cut them and the rest of the cheese into fine even slices.
6. Sprinkle it with fresh thyme and serve immediately.

: To roll out the dough more easily, place the ball of dough between two sheets of parchment paper before using the rolling pin.

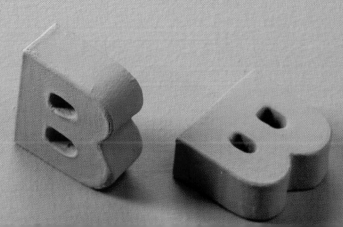

Open sea
sandwich

For 1 mom
Preparation time: 20 minutes
Cooking time: 10 minutes
Refrigeration time: 15 minutes

5 **frozen raw peeled shrimp**
1 **stem of lemongrass (optional)**
1 oz **canned crab legs**
1 **chive leaf (or garlic chives or scallion)**
1 **slice of purple onion**
2.5 oz **cottage cheese**
The juice from 1/2 a lime
Freshly ground pepper
Fleur de sel (or sea salt)
1 **slice wholegrain or wholewheat bread**

Virginie

During my pregnancy, I gorged myself on open sandwiches and simple snacks. This is refreshing, tangy and filling while still being light.

Paule

This open sandwich is perfect as a starter, and if you have a huge craving before a meal, it will help you to hang on. The protein from the shrimp and crab and the carbohydrate and fiber from the wholegrain bread are quite filling.

1. Fill the reservoir of your babycook with 3 measures of water. Place the shrimp in the steam basket and cook for 10 minutes.
2. If you have lemongrass, remove the first layer of skin and the green tip of the stem. Cut it into pieces and place them under the steam basket to flavor the shrimp. Leave them to cool.
3. In the meantime, shred the crabmeat and chop the chives finely, keeping as much green as possible. Cut the onion slice and the shrimp into small pieces.
4. Put the cottage cheese in a bowl and add the crab, chives, shrimp and purple onion.
5. Pour the lime juice over it and mix. Season to taste and refrigerate the mixture for 15 minutes.
6. Spread the mixture over a large slice of wholegrain bread.

Cupcakes
with white chocolate coulant centers

For about 6 cupcakes
Preparation time: 20 minutes
Cooking time: 15 minutes

2.5 oz 70% cocoa dark couverture (confectioner's grade) chocolate
2 eggs
0.75 oz (about 2 tbsp) granulated sugar
1 tbsp all-purpose flour
1.5 tbsp cornstarch
2 oz butter
1 tbsp cream
12 small white chocolate squares

1. Mix the eggs with the sugar in the babycook bowl before adding the flour and cornstarch. Pour the mixture into a mixing bowl.
2. Melt the chocolate in a bain marie (double boiler) with the butter and cream. Pour this mixture into the bowl and mix. Then place the bowl in the fridge until the mixture becomes firm.
3. Preheat the oven to 325°F.
4. Use a teaspoon to half fill six cupcake molds (paper or silicone). Place 2 white chocolate squares in the middle and cover them with the rest of the mixture.
5. Bake for 6 minutes and eat them straight away.

Virginie
And to continue not being sensible, dip your cupcake in a little custard.

Paule
Custard will give you calcium and protein, so – on the contrary – that's very sensible!

Dried fruit
sandwich spread

Virginie

Microwave this spread for a few seconds and have it warm at breakfast or tea.

Paule

Commercial spreads don't compare with this one that is full of minerals, especially magnesium. If you've been getting cramps, now is the time to make it!

For 1 mom
Preparation time: 10 minutes

4 **pitted dates**
2 **dried apricots**
3 **dried figs**
6 **dried cranberries**
4 tbsp **almond butter or hazelnut paste (health food shops)**
1 **slice raisin bread (or walnut or sesame bread)**

1. Cut the dried fruit into pieces and place them in the babycook bowl with almond butter. Blend it until you obtain the desired consistency.
2. Spread it over a lovely slice of raisin bread. Store in the refrigerator for up to 3 days.

Variation: You can also rehydrate dried fruit in your babycook. Fill the reservoir with 2 measures of water. Place the dried fruit in the steam basket and cook for 15 minutes. Once the fruit cools, blend it with the almond butter.

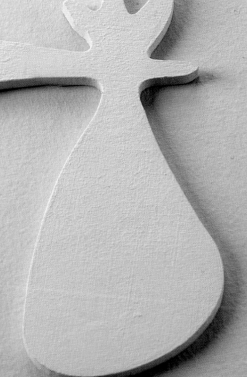

Pretty-in-pink
cheesecake

For 1 cheesecake
Preparation time: 30 minutes
Cooking time: 25 minutes
Refrigeration time: 12 hours

1 oz pink ladyfinger cookies
1 oz melted butter
3.5 oz ricotta cheese
3.5 oz cream cheese
1 oz (3 tbsp) granulated sugar
1 egg

1 tbsp rose syrup
1.75 oz rose petal jelly + **1 tbsp**
to decorate
1 tbsp crystallized rose petals
to decorate

Virginie

If you feel like a tangy flavor, replace the
pink cookies with lemon cookies and the
rose petal jelly with lemon curd, and add
the juice from 1/2 a lemon to the mixture.

Paule

A fruit salad with a slice of this cheesecake
will make a well-balanced dessert.

1. Preheat the oven to 350°F.

2. Chop the pink cookies coarsely in the babycook. Add melted butter and mix.

3. Line the base of springform cake pan with this mixture. Press it down well with a teaspoon. Place the cake pan in the freezer.

4. Blend the ricotta and the cream cheese together for 30 seconds in the babycook. Transfer this mixture to a mixing bowl and gently add the egg followed by the syrup. Add the rose petal jelly without mixing too much.

5. Pour this mixture into the cake pan and bake it in the oven for 25 minutes. The center of the cake should still be wobbly. Let the cheesecake cool in the oven with the door ajar, then refrigerate for 12 hours.

6. On the day, just before serving, spread a tbsp of rose petal jelly on the cheesecake and crumble the crystallized rose petals over it.

Banana
cookies

For 20 small cookies
Preparation time: 20 minutes
Cooking time: 8 minutes

1.75 oz **banana chips**
3.5 oz (just over 1/2 cup) **all-purpose flour**
2.5 oz **wholegrain muesli with dried fruit**
½ tsp **baking powder**
3.5 oz (just under 1/2 cup) **turbinado sugar**
2.5 oz **butter**
1 **egg**
1.75 oz **dried bananas**

1. Blend the banana chips in your babycook until they are reduced to a flour-like powder.
2. Mix the banana powder with the flour, muesli and baking powder in a mixing bowl.
3. Use another bowl to mix the sugar with the butter energetically until the mixture turns white. Then add the egg. Add this mixture to the first. Dice the dried bananas and add them. Mix everything together until it forms an even batter. Put it in the refrigerator. Preheat the oven to 325°F.
4. Make small walnut-sized balls and space them out every 2 inches on a baking sheet lined with parchment paper.
5. Bake them for 8 minutes in the oven. Leave them to solidify on a cake rack.

Virginie

I love these cookies. They're soft and crunchy at the same time, and not too sweet. Eat them to satisfy a small craving!

Paule

Satisfy that small craving with a glass of juice or fresh fruit smoothie (sugar-free obviously!) together with one or two of these delicious cookies that have quite a lot of minerals. This will also provide you with a lot of vitamins.

Index

THE EDITOR'S ACKNOWLEDGEMENTS

Thanks to Sophie Bunn, of the Béaba Company, and to all her team for accompanying us throughout the process of making this book.

THE AUTHOR'S ACKNOWLEDGEMENTS

Thank you

• to my three children Arthur, Charles and Louis who unwittingly inspired the recipes in this book.

• to my editor Alice and the Béaba brand for their trust and enthusiasm.

• to Françoise, my partner and talented photographer who made the experience of putting together the shots for this collection a happy one.

• a special thank you to Ressource Marchand de Couleurs et Décoration for their beautiful paint collections - S29, hC 89, F26, F37, I45, S39 - which feature as the backgrounds for this book.

www.ressource-peinture.com

THE PHOTOGRAPHER'S ACKNOWLEDGEMENTS

Thank you

• to Editions Culinaires and Alice in particular, for their professionalism and constant good humor.

• to Virginie for her unfailing good humor.

Collection Director
Emmanuel Jirou-Najou

Editor-in-chief
Alice Gouget

Editorial assistant
Claire Dupuy

Recipe creation and design
Virginie Michelin

Health consultant
Paule Neyrat

Photographs
Françoise Nicol

Graphic design
Anne Chaponnay

Layout
Cillero & de Motta

Translation
**Paula Pérez Yusta and Elena García Rubio
for Cillero & de Motta**

Photoengraving
Maury imprimeur

Partnership Manager
Alice Vasseur
alice.vasseur@alain-ducasse.com

Printing:
Printed in India, The Foundry USA

Legal deposit : 1st quartet 2011
ISBN : 978-2-84123-373-1
Copyright Lec. 2010
64 rue du Ranelagh
75016 Paris
www.cookboutic.fr